Copyright © 2025 by Rebel Girls, Inc.

Rebel Girls supports copyright. Copyright fuels creativity, encourages diverse voices, promotes free speech, and creates a vibrant culture. Thank you for buying an authorized edition of this book and for complying with copyright laws by not reproducing, scanning, or distributing any part of it in any form without permission. You are supporting indie creators as well as allowing Rebel Girls to publish books for Rebel Girls wherever they may be.

Good Night Stories for Rebel Girls and Rebel Girls are registered trademarks.
DK books are available at special discounts when purchased in bulk for sales promotions, premiums, fund-raising, or educational use. For details, contact:
DK Publishing Special Markets, 1745 Broadway, 20th Floor, New York, NY 10019
SpecialSales@dk.com

This is a work of creative nonfiction. It is a collection of heartwarming and thought-provoking stories inspired by the lives and adventures of 25 influential women. It is not an encyclopedic account of the events and accomplishments of their lives.

www.rebelgirls.com

Some of the artwork in this book has been previously published in the books *Good Night Stories for Rebel Girls*, *Good Night Stories for Rebel Girls 2*, *Good Night Stories for Rebel Girls: 100 Immigrant Women Who Changed the World*, *Good Night Stories for Rebel Girls: 100 Real-Life Tales of Black Girl Magic*, *Good Night Stories for Rebel Girls: 100 Inspiring Young Changemakers*, *Rebel Girls Awesome Entrepreneurs*, and *Rebel Girls Animal Allies*.

Library of Congress Control Number: 2023942023
Rebel Girls, Inc.
421 Elm Ave.
Larkspur, CA 94939

Text by Emma Carlson Berne, Margeaux Weston, Mel Hammond, Orli Zuravicky
Art direction by Giulia Flamini and Kristen Brittain
Cover illustrations by Joanne Dertili
Graphic design by Kristen Brittain
Edited by Eliza Kirby
Special thanks: Hannah Bennett, Jess Harriton, Sarah Parvis, Amy Pfister, Jes Wolfe, Anita Vandyke

Printed in China, 2024
10 9 8 7 6 5 4 3 2 1
001-341770-June'24
ISBN: 979-8-88964-099-8

CONTENTS

FOREWORD BY ANITA VANDYKE	4
ADA LOVELACE • Mathematician	6
ALICE MIN SOO CHUN • Inventor	8
ANGELINA TSUBOI • Programmer and Engineer	10
CORA RATTO DE SADOSKY • Mathematician and Activist	12
CYNTHIA BREAZEAL • Robotics Engineer and Entrepreneur	14
DARSHAN RANGANATHAN • Chemist	16
DASIA TAYLOR • Inventor	18
EMMA HARUKA IWAO • Computer Scientist	20
ETHELDRED BENETT • Geologist	22
FEI-FEI LI • Computer Scientist	24
IRENE UCHIDA • Geneticist	26
KARLIE NOON • Astronomer	28
KATHERINE JOHNSON • Computer Scientist	30
LYNN CONWAY • Computer Scientist and Engineer	32
MARCELA TORRES • Founder and Social Scientist	34
MEGAN SMITH • Engineer and Technologist	36
MELANIA ALVAREZ • Mathematics Educator	38
NASIM AMIRALIAN • Scientist and Engineer	40
NGALULA SANDRINE MUBENGA • Electrical Engineer	42
NICOLE AUNAPU MANN • Astronaut	44
NKECHI AGWU • Ethnomathematician	46
REBECCA LEE CRUMPLER • Doctor	48
ROSE LEKE • Immunologist	50
SOPHIE GERMAIN • Mathematician	52
VALENTINA MUÑOZ RABANAL • Activist and Programmer	54
MEET MORE REBELS	56
KEEP INNOVATING	60
THE ILLUSTRATORS	66
MORE BOOKS!	67
ABOUT REBEL GIRLS	68

FOREWORD

Dear Rebels,

As long as I can remember, I have gazed at the stars and wondered how I could reach them. The sense of mystery, the exploration of the unknown, and the amazing possibility of venturing into the final frontier was embedded into me as a young girl living in Sydney, Australia.

That continued sense of adventure is why I went on to study aeronautical space engineering at university. I wanted to be a rocket scientist so I could solve problems and (literally) reach for the stars. I worked hard and when I was 16 years old, I won a national science competition to see rocket launches in outback Australia. That ignited my passion even more!

As a girl in science and technology, I had to overcome many hurdles. I was one of two women from my university who graduated with my degree, and women continue to be a minority in most engineering fields. But that didn't deter me from my dream of becoming a rocket scientist. I had a passion for astronomy, science, and math.

After I became a rocket scientist, I worked on aircraft all around Australia, with the goal of eventually becoming an astronaut. But something happened along the way. I realized that the greatest service I could do was to stay grounded here on Earth and look after the only planet we can call home. I went back to school to study to become a medical doctor, and now I work with patients to make their daily lives better. That doesn't mean I've lost my passion for the stars. I still aim to combine my passions in the future. Maybe one day I will work in aerospace medicine. And that's what I want to remind you: to follow your heart and be of service to the world. With those two goals, you'll never go wrong.

My story is not dissimilar to yours or the stories of many other amazing women who have tackled new frontiers in science and technology. You'll read about a few of them in this book. Some of these names might be familiar to you, like mathematician Ada Lovelace and NASA computer scientist Katherine Johnson. Some of the others you may be hearing about for the first time, like Rose Leke, who works to cure malaria across the continent of Africa, and Alice Min Soo Chun, who invented a portable solar light inspired by origami. For all of us, the main driver is that we have ambition and are resilient. We are not scared to tackle the unknown, and that's what makes us great doctors, scientists, and engineers.

We need more young girls who aren't afraid to shoot for the stars, and I hope this book inspires you to be one of them.

—Dr. Anita Vandyke

SCAN TO HEAR MORE!

BONUS! AUDiO STORiES!
Download the Rebel Girls app to unlock creative activities and discover stories of trailblazing women. When you come across a beaker icon, scan the code, and you'll be whisked away on an audio adventure.

ADA LOVELACE

MATHEMATICIAN

SCAN TO HEAR MORE!

Many years ago in England, there was a young girl named Ada who was excellent at math. Ada lived during a time when girls were supposed to become wives and mothers—not scientists or mathematicians. Ada's mother loved math and science, though, and made sure Ada learned both subjects. But one thing her mother did not like was imagination. When Ada was too curious or creative, her mother put a stop to it. Still, Ada loved discovering how things worked. She was mesmerized by the way colors reflected off of water and the way birds flew through the sky. Ada even began inventing a pair of silk wings so she could fly too.

As an adult, Ada met a mathematician named Charles Babbage. He had invented a machine called the Difference Engine that could solve math problems on its own, like a modern-day calculator. He was working on a new invention, the Analytical Engine, that would be able to do even more. Ada began helping Charles and soon realized the possibilities. She believed the Analytical Engine could be used to understand not only numbers but words and pictures too. She even thought it could play music!

Ada wrote down her own thoughts and ideas about the machine. Eventually, her notes were published in a scientific journal. In her most famous note, she explained how the machine could follow step-by-step instructions to make something happen. These instructions are called an algorithm. Today, computer programs and apps use algorithms all the time. This imaginative scientific discovery crowned Ada the first ever computer programmer.

DECEMBER 10, 1815 – NOVEMBER 27, 1852

UNITED KINGDOM

ALICE MIN SOO CHUN
INVENTOR

There once was a young girl named Alice who loved to build things. Her mother taught her origami, the Japanese art of folding paper into shapes. One of the things she tried to make was a balloon. It took Alice many days to learn how to fold the paper just right. She crumpled sheet after sheet until finally, she mastered the creases. When she was done, she softly blew air into a small hole, and the paper inflated just like a real balloon!

Years later, Alice became an architect and a teacher. One day, she took her son to the doctor and found out he had asthma. Alice was worried. Her son was not alone though. There were lots of children in the doctor's office. *Why do so many children have trouble breathing?* she asked herself. Alice began to research. She learned that our air has a lot of pollution in it from burning fossil fuels, like oil, for energy. She also discovered that in places without electricity, millions of people were burning a dangerous and expensive oil called kerosene just to have light. Alice couldn't believe it.

She began to build a special light powered by the sun that people without electricity could use safely. Inspired by the origami balloons she had learned to make as a child, she designed the SolarPuff™ light to be a similar shape: it could inflate and deflate with the help of a pull tab. That made it easy to store and travel with.

Alice went all over the world, bringing thousands of her portable lights to places where children were living through hardships like wars and earthquakes. Because of Alice's invention, many more kids can see and breathe safely.

BORN 1965
SOUTH KOREA AND UNITED STATES OF AMERICA

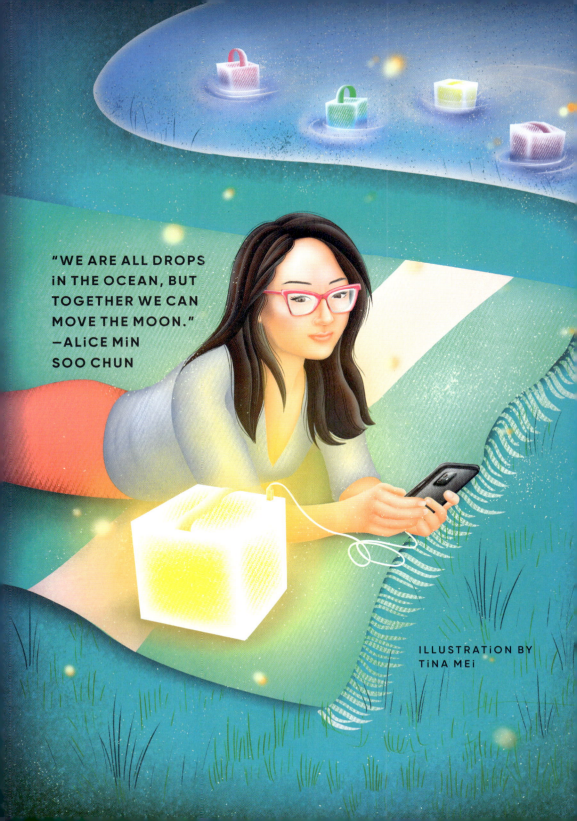

ANGELiNA TSUBOi

PROGRAMMER AND ENGiNEER

Once a girl named Angelina found a broken-down refrigerator in a parking lot. With help from her two brothers, she dragged it to her backyard and took it apart. As she examined each piece, Angelina began to understand how the machine worked. She never forgot the joy of discovering something new—even though her mom was pretty upset about the fridge in their yard.

When Angelina turned seven, she learned to program a simple maze game on the computer. After that, she worked on project after project, and her coding skills got better and better. By the time she was 17, she had learned 17 programming languages and invented another one herself!

With everything she does, Angelina makes the world a better place. She's built tools that help people learn CPR, predict tsunamis, and monitor air quality. One special project was inspired by her mom. After Angelina's mother immigrated to the US from Japan, she had a tough time finding childcare and housing because she didn't speak English. *There has to be a way to help*, Angelina thought. So she created an app that helps single parents like her mom find jobs, nannies, housing, and translators.

For Angelina, learning about a problem and coming up with creative ways to solve it is exciting. "It feels almost like an adventure," she says. And as if problem-solving wasn't adventure enough, Angelina learned to fly an airplane! When she soars above fluffy white clouds, she gets a new perspective on the world. And, of course, as she went through flight training, she used her coding to help others along the way. She developed an app to help budding aviators fly the skies.

BORN MARCH 15, 2006
UNiTED STATES OF AMERiCA

CORA RATTO DE SADOSKY

MATHEMATICIAN AND ACTIVIST

Once upon a time in Argentina, South America, there was a young girl named Cora who loved math. She loved it so much that she planned to be a math teacher when she grew up. She hoped to inspire and encourage other students to love math too.

When Cora was old enough, she went to the University of Buenos Aires to get her math degree. While she was focused on her studies, the world outside the classroom was changing. World War II was beginning in Europe. Like much of the world, Cora did not approve of the German government. Cora was devoted to math, but she was also passionate about justice. She believed that all people should be treated equally and spoke out against laws and governments that she thought were unfair.

As the war continued, Cora started a special women's organization called *La Junta de la Victoria*, or the Victory Union, to fight against Nazi Germany. La Junta grew to be the biggest women's organization ever to exist in Latin America.

Years later, after Cora got married and had a daughter, she returned to studying math. Finally, she became a math professor! Cora was energetic, witty, and caring, and her students adored her. During her time teaching, Cora cowrote a math textbook. It was the first of its kind written in Spanish.

Cora's love of math and justice came together when she formed the Albert Einstein Foundation. She wanted students all over Argentina to have the same opportunity to learn as she had, no matter who they were or how much money they had. Her foundation helped many diverse young mathematicians get an education in math and science.

JANUARY 3, 1912 – JANUARY 2, 1981

ARGENTINA

"BY HELPING THE BRAVE SOLDIERS OF LIBERTY, WE HELP OUR OWN SELVES."
—CORA RATTO DE SADOSKY

ILLUSTRATION BY VALERIA ARAYA

CYNTHIA BREAZEAL

ROBOTICS ENGINEER AND ENTREPRENEUR

When Cynthia first saw *Star Wars* while growing up in northern California, she wanted to step into space along with the fearless characters. But it wasn't the heroic Luke Skywalker or the brave Princess Leia who caught her attention. It was the robots. C-3PO and R2-D2 seemed like friends. *Why can't we have robots like that in real life?* Cynthia asked herself.

Both of Cynthia's parents were computer scientists, so Cynthia was used to thinking about technology. Her family had a personal computer before anyone else she knew. Cynthia's mom and dad took her and her brother to science events around the city. When Cynthia went to college, majoring in computer engineering felt like being back at home.

Later, Cynthia went to work at the MIT Media Lab, one of the most famous computer labs in the world. She designed robots that could move around on other planets. But after a while, Cynthia wondered, *Why are the robots being sent into space or the ocean? Why aren't there robots in our own homes?* She remembered how R2-D2 and C-3PO got along with humans like buddies.

She realized she wanted to invent a robot that could respond to people's feelings. That way, Cynthia thought, the robot could be like a teammate. She got to work in her lab. Eventually, Jibo was born. It was a little white robot that sat on a counter. It could take pictures, and it used its kind voice to answer questions, read stories, and remind people of their appointments. Cynthia started a company to sell Jibo to the world.

Cynthia believes that robots can make human lives better. That's a lesson she learned while watching *Star Wars* in that dark California movie theater. She's never forgotten it.

BORN NOVEMBER 15, 1967
UNITED STATES OF AMERICA

DARSHAN RANGANATHAN
CHEMiST

Once upon a time in the vibrant, bustling city of Delhi, India, there was a curious young girl named Darshan who loved to solve problems. When she grew up, Darshan decided to learn about chemistry—the study of different substances' properties and how they behave. Soon she got a huge opportunity: she was chosen to work in a lab in London, halfway across the world. She studied how large molecules called proteins behaved in fruit. But Darshan had one problem.

In India, she'd used jackfruit in her research. The stringy fruit was common where Darshan grew up. But in London, it was nowhere to be found. *How can I keep studying without it?* she wondered. Ever the problem-solver, Darshan had an idea. She asked her mom to send her dried jackfruit all the way from Delhi! Her quick thinking allowed her to continue her research and discover new ways to work with proteins.

Darshan moved back to India to work as a college professor. She had earned many awards and wanted to inspire the next generation of women scientists. But when Darshan applied for a permanent job at the college, she was turned down. It wasn't that she was a bad fit for the position. An unofficial rule prevented women from working with their husbands. Since her husband was already a professor there, that meant Darshan couldn't be hired.

Angry and disappointed, Darshan was faced with another problem: how could she afford to continue her research without the college's help? She decided to pay for it herself. She earned money to fund her research and spoke at schools across the country. By using her creativity to find solutions, Darshan became one of the most successful chemists in India.

JUNE 4, 1941–JUNE 4, 2001
INDiA

ILLUSTRATION BY
TRISHA SRIVASTAVA

DASIA TAYLOR

INVENTOR

Growing up as an only child, Dasia spent a lot of time inventing things. She even created her own spy gadgets! Although Dasia was always creating, she wasn't interested in science until her chemistry teacher encouraged her to enter her high school's science fair. She may not have been sure about science, but Dasia *was* sure that she wanted to help others.

While doing research one day, Dasia learned something that changed her life. After surgeries, doctors look for signs of infection, like redness and swelling. But these signs are often harder to see on darker skin. That puts some patients in danger. Dasia put her problem-solving skills to work.

She tested sutures, the stitches that hold wounds together. She found that sutures coated in beet juice would change colors—from bright red to dark purple—when a wound became infected. Dasia's new sutures would make it easy to tell if there was an infection no matter the color of a patient's skin. They would also be much less expensive than other similar sutures, making them more accessible to everyone. She showcased her discovery at the science fair, and to her surprise, she won her first competition. Then another, and another!

She advanced to the final stage of the biggest STEM competition for young people in the United States, competing against nearly 2,000 students. Dasia was a finalist in the competition, and soon her life-saving invention got even more attention. She went on TV shows and talked about her discovery. It seemed like everyone wanted to know about her amazing sutures.

After graduation, Dasia started a medical device company and now mentors STEM students. She says, "My hope is that young people everywhere can have the opportunity to experience STEM."

BORN AUGUST 2, 2003

UNITED STATES OF AMERICA

EMMA HARUKA IWAO

COMPUTER SCiENTiST

Once upon a time in Japan, a 12-year-old girl named Emma got curious about a number. The number was called pi. It started with 3.14 and then it just kept going with decimal numbers in tinier and tinier amounts. No one knew where pi ended. Emma downloaded a program on her computer that could calculate pi. She'd heard about a computer scientist named Daisuke Takahashi who had used a computer to calculate about two and a half trillion digits of pi. *Could I break Daisuke's record?* Emma asked herself.

Emma became a computer scientist and started working with a powerful set of computer programs. *How much can this platform do?* Emma wondered. She decided to test it on her old friend pi. Emma used a special program to calculate 31.4 trillion digits of pi. It was a new world record!

Three years later, a team of researchers broke that record, but there were still more numbers to be revealed. Emma decided it was time for another challenge. This time, she would try to calculate pi to 100 trillion digits. If she could do it, she would break the new record.

So Emma made some changes and ran the program again. For almost 158 days, it worked and worked, collecting giant amounts of data. Then, finally, it spat out the number. That number was so long that if Emma were to read it out loud, it would take her 3.1 million years.

Emma showed the world that clever computer programmers could enable fast, powerful computers to do amazing things. "This is my childhood dream," Emma said. "And making the dream come true twice is a really great honor for me." She hadn't reached the end of pi, but she'd gotten further than anyone else.

BORN APRIL 22, 1984
JAPAN

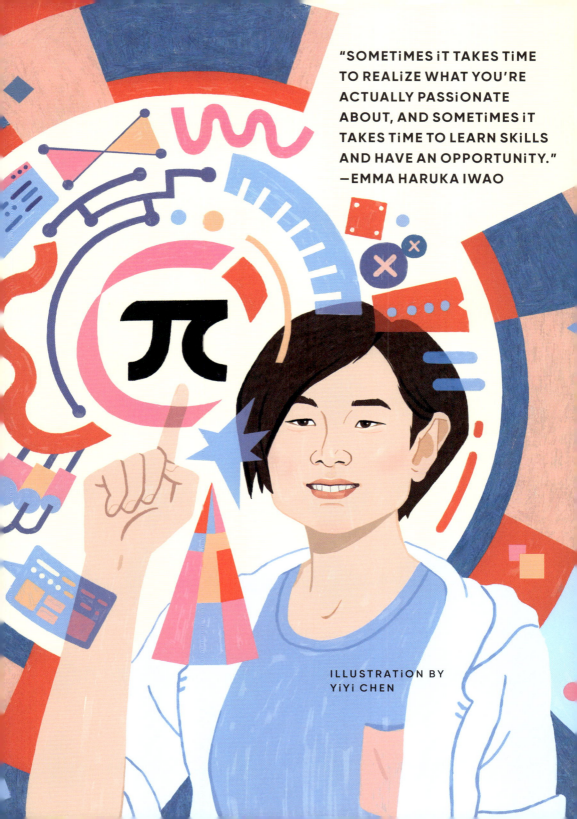

ETHELDRED BENETT
GEOLOGIST

Long ago, there was a girl with the unusual name of Etheldred. She grew up in a wealthy family and never got married, which meant she had plenty of time and money to do whatever she liked. And she liked to collect fossils.

Digging in the cool, damp dirt in the fields around her home in England, Etheldred uncovered bones of dinosaurs and mammoths that stomped around the Earth millions of years ago. She dug up traces of extinct sea creatures, like urchins, coral, crabs, and sponges. People came from miles away to visit her impressive collection.

Not everyone took Etheldred's work seriously. Because she was a woman, she wasn't welcome in the Geological Society of London, where scientists who studied the Earth met and shared ideas. Sometimes other geologists even stole her discoveries and passed them off as their own. *She's not a real geologist—she's just a collector,* they'd say.

Because her name was similar to a common boy's name, Etheldred exchanged letters with many geologists who assumed she was a man. Once, the emperor of Russia was so impressed with Etheldred's work that he sent her a diploma from the University of St. Petersburg. When she opened it, the title *Dominum* appeared in front of her name, which is an old-fashioned way of addressing a man. At that time, women weren't allowed to attend that school!

Etheldred's collection grew to more than 1,500 fossils, including some species that hadn't yet been discovered. To make sure that geologists remembered her work, she published her discoveries in a book. She had started collecting fossils just for fun. But today, people believe she may have been the world's first female geologist.

JULY 22, 1776 – JANUARY 11, 1845

UNITED KINGDOM

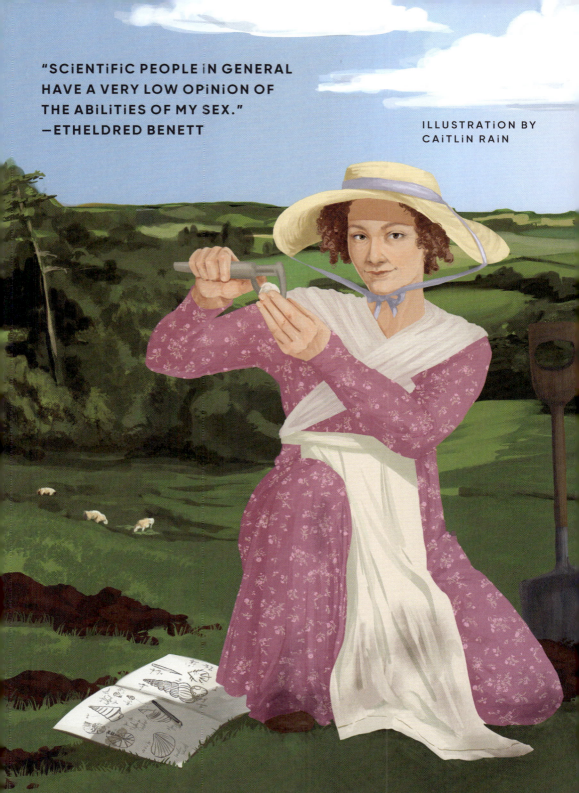

"SCIENTIFIC PEOPLE IN GENERAL HAVE A VERY LOW OPINION OF THE ABILITIES OF MY SEX."
—ETHELDRED BENETT

ILLUSTRATION BY CAITLIN RAIN

FEI-FEI LI

COMPUTER SCIENTIST

Fei-Fei was always a scientist at heart. As a kid, she loved reading books about life, space, and the universe, and searching for the truth about the world around her. Born in China, Fei-Fei and her family moved to America when she was a teenager. Being an immigrant was hard and often lonely. In order to help her family and pay for college, Fei-Fei borrowed money so her parents could buy a dry cleaning shop, which she ran on the weekends. After years of hard work and studying, Fei-Fei's dream of being a scientist came true.

Fei-Fei studied a type of computer technology called artificial intelligence, or AI. AI is the science of teaching computers how to understand the world the way a person can. Computers can do lots of complicated things, but they aren't as smart as people. Fei-Fei knew that her three-year-old son could already understand and describe the things he saw around him better than a computer could.

That's when she realized something big: *no one teaches a child how to see—they learn through real-world experiences*. She needed to figure out a way to show the computer as much of the real world as her son saw during his first three years of life. So Fei-Fei and her team showed the computer millions and millions of photos—more photos than any computer had processed before. She and her team labeled them all.

Her theory worked! The computer learned to recognize objects more often than it had before. It even learned how to see a picture and compose a full sentence about it, just like her son could. There's still a lot for Fei-Fei and other scientists to teach computers, but the work she's done so far is making technology better every day.

BORN 1976

CHINA AND UNITED STATES OF AMERICA

"I THINK THERE IS SOMETHING BEAUTIFUL ABOUT THE PURSUIT OF TRUTH."
—FEI-FEI LI

ILLUSTRATION BY KIMBERLIE CLINTHORNE-WONG

IRENE UCHIDA

GENETICIST

It was November of 1941. Irene had just arrived home to Canada after a long trip to Japan. World War II was in full swing, and Irene was able to make it out on the last boat leaving Yokohama. But when she got back, she was met with terrible news. Some people were afraid that Japanese Canadians like her might be helping the enemy in the war. So the government made the cruel decision to put thousands of ordinary citizens into internment camps, which were usually reserved for prisoners of war.

Irene, her family, and more than 20,000 other Japanese Canadians were forced to leave their homes and jobs and live in cramped, unsafe quarters. Irene's camp was filled with frightened families with young children. She began teaching the kids and took an interest in what made each one different.

After the war, Irene studied genetics—the science of the genes kids inherit from their parents. Genes control eye color, hair color, and sometimes what diseases people get. She opened a lab to research disorders like Down syndrome, which can happen when someone is born with an extra chromosome. Chromosomes are the tiny building blocks inside every person that contain their genes. When someone is born with an extra one, they look and act different from people who have the typical amount. *What if those extra chromosomes could be detected before a baby was born?* Irene wondered.

Irene worked hard to develop a test for chromosome numbers. With Irene's test, parents could learn more about their baby's genes—even before the baby was born! She also determined that radiation, like X-rays, could cause Down syndrome. These discoveries changed the way doctors care for pregnant people and their babies. Irene encouraged scientists to "find every possible way to help people."

APRIL 8, 1917–JULY 30, 2013

CANADA

KARLiE NOON

ASTRONOMER

As an Aboriginal girl, Karlie grew up hearing amazing stories about her ancestors' achievements. She knew they'd made great discoveries in astronomy and amazing inventions like the boomerang, but she rarely learned about them in school. In Australia, where she lived, Aboriginal contributions were all around her, but they were frequently overlooked. Sometimes she felt like her culture was invisible.

In her small Australian town, Karlie struggled to fit in. She grew up speaking Kamilaroi and Wiradjuri, Indigenous languages. At school, some kids picked on her because she was poor and didn't have clean clothes to wear. Karlie spent more time at home than at school. But with the help of a family friend, Karlie began to take an interest in studying and developed a love of math. She eventually became the first Indigenous woman in Australia to graduate with a double degree in math and science.

Soon Karlie began working in astronomy and mentoring Indigenous kids in STEM programs. She teaches them how to incorporate their culture into research and problem-solving and encourages them to shoot for the stars, just like she did. She wants to show the world how incredible her Indigenous culture is.

Looking up at the night sky, Karlie points out the moon's halo. She shows students how her Aboriginal ancestors paid attention to the number of stars between the moon and the edge of its halo to determine how soon a storm would come. Karlie's research shines a light on Aboriginal discoveries and how ancient wisdom and modern science work together. After growing up feeling invisible, Karlie makes sure that her culture is always seen.

BORN AUGUST 14, 1990

AUSTRALiA

ILLUSTRATION BY STORY HEMI-MOREHOUSE

KATHERINE JOHNSON

COMPUTER SCIENTIST

From a young age, Katherine was obsessed with numbers. When her family sat down for a meal, she counted how many plates were on the table. When she went somewhere, she counted the exact number of steps it took to get there. One day, at four years old, she marched 97 steps to her older brother Charlie's school and told his teacher she was there to help him with his math—and that's exactly what she did!

Katherine whizzed through school thanks to her special abilities in math. Soon she became one of the first Black women to work as a "computer" for the National Advisory Committee for Aeronautics, now called NASA. The computers we have today didn't exist back then. Instead, "computers" were real people who solved math problems by hand. All day long, Katherine counted and calculated. She did well and was quickly promoted. At that time, Black people were often treated poorly, and women were regularly excluded in the workplace. Katherine was the only woman—Black or white—who was allowed to sit in on certain important meetings.

When NASA announced a mission to send men to the moon, they asked Katherine for help. She had to determine the path the spaceship would take to land on the moon and come back to Earth safely. Katherine counted and calculated some more. Her numbers had to be exact. One wrong calculation could mean danger for the astronauts.

On the day of the launch, Katherine watched on the edge of her seat as the Apollo 11 spacecraft blasted off. Were her calculations right? Just as she had when she was a little girl, Katherine had computed the numbers perfectly. The mission was a big success!

AUGUST 26, 1918 – FEBRUARY 24, 2020

UNITED STATES OF AMERICA

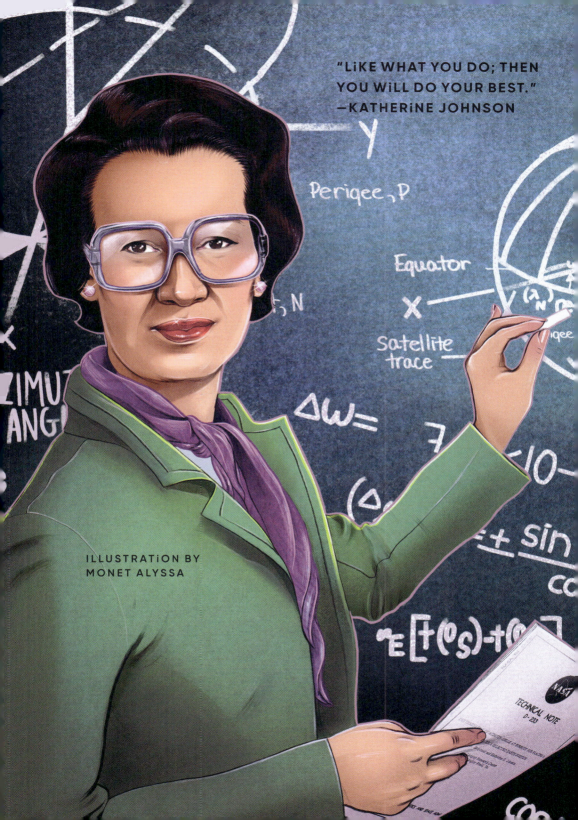

LYNN CONWAY

COMPUTER SCiENTiST AND ENGiNEER

Growing up, Lynn loved listening to the radio. *How does this incredible machine work?* she wondered. She wanted to take the radio apart and examine its tubes and wires. When her father gave her a big book about how the world worked, Lynn started reading about electricity, radios, and engineering. Becoming an engineer felt like the perfect fit.

But another part of Lynn's life did not feel like a perfect fit. When she was born, the doctors said she was a boy, but she knew she was a girl. She had to keep her identity a secret, though, and live as a boy. It could be hard and dangerous to come out as transgender. Trans people sometimes faced violence or lost their jobs because of who they were.

After college, Lynn became a computer scientist and an engineer. She went to work for IBM, a major computer company. Lynn loved her work making computers run better and faster. But she did not love hiding her gender identity. Finally, she decided to live as the person she had always known she was.

When Lynn told IBM she was transitioning, they fired her. She was angry but determined to keep doing the work she loved. With her new name and identity, she went to work at a different company. No one there knew anything about her past—Lynn felt safer keeping it private.

Lynn designed microchips and other computer parts and systems. She taught classes and won awards. She was doing everything she'd ever dreamed of as a computer scientist and engineer. Finally, Lynn decided that she felt safe telling the world she was trans. Fifty-two years after firing her, IBM apologized. And Lynn spoke out in support of other trans people, especially teenagers. They should be able to live their authentic lives, just like her.

JANUARY 2, 1938–JUNE 9, 2024
UNiTED STATES OF AMERiCA

"IF YOU WANT TO CHANGE THE FUTURE, START LIVING AS IF YOU'RE ALREADY THERE."
—LYNN CONWAY

ILLUSTRATION BY VERONICA JOHNSON

MARCELA TORRES

FOUNDER AND SOCIAL SCIENTIST

In a bustling city in Mexico built on top of a lake, there was a young woman named Marcela who wanted to solve a big problem in her country. Marcela loved computers and technology. She also loved studying people and populations.

Marcela noticed that there was a new generation of Mexicans who were born in Mexico but raised in America. When they came back to Mexico as young adults, they had a hard time. Many of them didn't even speak Spanish. Instead of feeling as if they had come home, they felt like strangers in a strange place. Marcela noticed something else too: Mexico had a lot of available jobs for people who could develop computer programs and technology but not a lot of people who actually had those skills. A light bulb switched on in her head!

So Marcela started Hola<Code/>, a special school where returning Mexicans could learn technology skills like coding and building computer applications. Hola<Code/> helped them pick up the skills they needed for all of those open jobs that Marcela had noticed. It was also a place for students to meet new people and become part of a community. Marcela made sure Hola<Code/> helped students pay for things they needed while they were in school. It also helped them find jobs when they graduated.

Starting a technology business in Mexico as a woman was challenging, so Marcela made a point of supporting other young women who wanted to do the same. Thanks to Marcela's work, Mexicans who came back after living abroad could really feel like they were returning home.

BORN APRIL 23, 1987
MEXICO

MEGAN SMITH

ENGINEER AND TECHNOLOGIST

For Megan's eighth-grade science fair, every student in the school was required to do a project that tackled a real-world issue. Where to start? Megan saw issues all around her through her mom's work on the first Earth Day and her dad's work on equal housing. The river that ran through her hometown of Buffalo, New York, was so polluted that it had once caught on fire. And nearby, a toxic waste dump leaked chemicals into the water and made kids sick. She saw US President Jimmy Carter adding solar panels to the White House roof and decided to explore green energy.

During the science fair, Megan proudly shared her design for a solar-powered house. But she wasn't the only student with plans for helping the planet. The room was full of new perspectives. Megan never forgot the power of listening to other people's ideas. She grew up to design all sorts of machines and solutions with her friends, like a solar-powered car that raced 3,000 miles across Australia and one of the first smartphones. But no matter the project, Megan always invited many people to the brainstorming table. "With seven billion people on the planet, someone around here probably has a solution to just about everything," she says.

In 2014, Megan received an unexpected email. President Barack Obama wanted her to join his team as the chief technology officer of the United States. In that role, Megan helped the country deal with big issues, like how to make laws about new technology. And she organized programs to get more kids into STEM, especially girls. She keeps encouraging kids from all genders, races, and backgrounds to use technology to solve the world's problems. The more teammates and ideas, the better!

BORN 1964
UNITED STATES OF AMERICA

MELANIA ALVAREZ

MATHEMATICS EDUCATOR

There once was a girl named Melania who grew up in Mexico City. Her family expected her to get married, have kids, and live nearby. But Melania had big dreams to study math, travel, and make a difference.

Melania did get married and have kids, but she also became a mathematician and moved to the US and then Canada. Her kids loved math too. That's why Melania was surprised when her son's middle school placed him in a low-level math class. His teachers expected him to be bad at math because he was Latino. Melania was furious.

Her son wasn't alone. Melania noticed that many kids didn't get the education they deserved because their teachers wrongly assumed they were bad at math. This problem especially affected Indigenous students—those whose ancestors were native to North America. Even worse, some of these students expected math to be difficult and boring. *I have to do something,* Melania thought.

So Melania gathered math puzzles, games, and art projects and invited students to play with them. Afterward, she asked, "Did you have a good time?"

"Yes!" they screamed.

"So you all love math?" she asked.

The students looked confused. "No!" they replied.

Melania said, "What are you talking about? You've been doing math for the last hour and a half!" The students were shocked. Could math really be fun?

Since then, Melania has spent decades running fun-filled math workshops and summer camps. Because of her, more Indigenous students have graduated high school, gone on to study math in college, and gotten the jobs they dreamed of. Melania defied people's expectations of her, and she's spent her career helping others do the same.

BORN JUNE 21, 1960
MEXICO AND CANADA

NASIM AMIRALIAN

SCIENTIST AND ENGINEER

There once was a girl named Nasim who wanted a PhD, the highest degree someone can earn at a university. While she applied to schools, she got a job at a fabric factory. She worked hard there, but daydreams of being a scientist and running experiments filled her mind. For years, school after school rejected her. But Nasim was strong. She didn't give up on her goal.

Finally, a school accepted her. Nasim flew from Iran to Queensland, Australia. It was heartbreaking to leave her friends and family behind. Plus, adjusting to life in a new country turned out to be tough. But Nasim was tougher.

At her university, Nasim studied a desert grass called spinifex. Aboriginal people, whose ancestors have always lived in Australia, had been using this grass for thousands of years to build shelters, weave baskets, and make glue. Working with Aboriginal people, Nasim discovered that spinifex contained tiny strands 10,000 times thinner than human hairs but eight times stronger than steel. These strands could be made into bioplastic, plastic that comes from plants and doesn't pollute the Earth. That meant Nasim could use spinifex to make disposable gloves and packaging that were Earth-friendly and strong.

These strands didn't exist only in desert grass. Nasim also found them in plant waste like the rinds and peels of pineapples, bananas, and sugarcane, all of which grow in Australia. Not only is Nasim reusing plant waste and reducing plastic trash, but she's also making products that are stronger than ever—as strong as the woman who flew across the world to achieve her goals.

BORN AUGUST 19, 1981
IRAN AND AUSTRALIA

NGALULA SANDRINE MUBENGA

ELECTRICAL ENGINEER

At 17, Ngalula found herself alone in a dark hospital room in her hometown of Kikwit in the Democratic Republic of the Congo. She needed emergency surgery to remove her appendix, but the hospital had no power. Not only that, but the backup generators—gas-powered mobile machines used to produce power—could not be used because the whole city was out of fuel.

After three days of waiting, Ngalula finally had the life-saving procedure. The frightening experience inspired her to learn how she could help people who did not have reliable access to electricity.

Ngalula became a professor of electrical engineering at the University of Toledo in Ohio. She invented a machine to make batteries in electric vehicles, planes, and electricity stations last longer. The technology she developed could help people around the world. But creating it wasn't easy. Ngalula had to sketch out models on paper and a computer and do several rounds of testing. There were even times when wires burned and sparks flew! Ngalula didn't give up. She knew that finding ways to create long-lasting energy could save someone's life.

Later, Ngalula founded a company that develops and installs solar panels across her home country. The solar panels convert sunlight into electrical energy. With each roof her team fills with solar panels, Ngalula hopes she can keep more people safe and healthy. The girl who once lay afraid in a dark hospital now works hard to make sure the lights never go out.

BORN MAY 15, 1980
DEMOCRATIC REPUBLIC OF THE CONGO AND
UNITED STATES OF AMERICA

NICOLE AUNAPU MANN
ASTRONAUT

Once there was a girl named Nicole who had a lot of trouble sleeping. Night after night, bad dreams flooded her head, keeping her from peaceful slumber. One day, her mother gave her a gift. Nicole and her family were Native American, part of the Wailaki of the Round Valley nation in California. The gift was a special Native American object called a dream catcher. Her mother said it would catch the bad dreams in its web and let only the good ones into Nicole's head. Picturing that made her feel strong and protected.

As Nicole grew up, the strength and safety she felt helped her succeed at many things, especially her studies. She did well in math and science, and she got a degree in engineering. Then Nicole began training at NASA to be an astronaut. She did so well, she was chosen to be the commander of the SpaceX Crew-5 mission.

When Nicole and her crew launched into the sky, she became the first Native American woman ever to go into space. She was proud to represent her community. She hoped her work would inspire Native American kids and help them realize that they too could achieve great things.

The crew's mission was to live on a special space station and do all kinds of science experiments to figure out how humans can live in space and on other planets like Mars. They were even able to grow tomatoes in space! Although Nicole was far away from her family and the Wailaki community, she brought a piece of home with her. The dream catcher her mother had given her so long ago floated around Nicole's cabin on the space station, ready to protect her from bad dreams, give her strength, and remind her that she is loved.

BORN JUNE 27, 1977
UNITED STATES OF AMERICA

"SEEING EARTH FROM SPACE GIVES YOU THIS AMAZING PERSPECTIVE AND APPRECIATION FOR WHAT WE HAVE."
—NICOLE AUNAPU MANN

ILLUSTRATION BY STORY HEMI-MOREHOUSE

NKECHI AGWU

ETHNOMATHEMATICIAN

Once upon a time, there was a girl who found math all around her. Born in Nigeria, Nkechi spent some of her childhood living in refugee camps across West Africa. A refugee camp is a place for people who have to leave their home country because it is no longer safe. Although times were challenging for her family, Nkechi kept herself entertained in each new place she moved. She loved using math in clever ways, finding patterns to make dolls and play mancala, an African board game. Nkechi realized that no matter where she was, math was always there.

Nkechi studied math in school, and when she got older, she moved to America to learn more. She was excited to be in a new country with new opportunities, but things were different there. Nkechi was the only Black person—and the only woman—in her program. This was different from her experiences at African schools, where she was always around students who looked like her. She felt disappointed that there weren't more people of color in math. She knew she wanted to encourage Black women to pursue mathematics degrees.

Now Nkechi teaches and mentors women and underrepresented students in STEM. She teaches her students how math plays a role in their cultures and communities. From simple games and African doll-making to textile design and architecture, math is everywhere, connecting people all over the world. Nkechi wants students to understand how math can be used in all aspects of their lives—just like she learned as a child in the refugee camps.

BORN OCTOBER 8, 1962

NIGERIA AND UNITED STATES OF AMERICA

REBECCA LEE CRUMPLER

DOCTOR

Many years ago, a girl named Rebecca grew up with a kind aunt who knew about medicine. Back then, many doctors refused to treat Black patients, so neighbors helped each other. When someone got sick, Rebecca helped her aunt take good care of them.

When she got older, Rebecca worked as a nurse for eight years. Then she had a bold idea: why not become a doctor? At the time, there were 54,000 doctors in the United States, and only 300 of them were women. None of these women were Black. Not only did Rebecca get accepted to an all-white medical school, but she also became the first Black woman in the country to earn a medical degree!

When the Civil War ended, Rebecca moved to Virginia to help care for Black people who were finally free from slavery. Being a Black woman doctor wasn't easy. Other doctors ridiculed her. Pharmacists refused to give her the medicine she asked for. Hospitals wouldn't let her bring her patients inside. But Rebecca did whatever it took to help sick people in need. And when her patients couldn't pay, she worked for free.

At the end of her career, Rebecca wrote a book that taught women how to treat illnesses and care for their children. It was likely the first medical book written by a Black person. Rebecca believed that if people understood how their bodies worked, they could better care for each other—just like her aunt had taught her. Long after her death, Rebecca's book continued to spread good health throughout her community.

FEBRUARY 8, 1831 – MARCH 9, 1895

UNiTED STATES OF AMERiCA

ROSE LEKE

IMMUNOLOGIST

When Rose was a little girl in Cameroon, she thought getting sick often was a normal part of life. A few times a year, her family caught malaria, a life-threatening disease that causes dangerously high fevers. The weekly medicine they got from the local clinic didn't stop them from falling ill. Rose's mother used herbs like lemongrass to help the family recover more quickly. As Rose grew older, she realized that she could help prevent people from being sick all the time.

Rose set out to make her community safer and healthier by becoming an expert in diseases. She studied how diseases spread and how each disease affects the immune system. Then she used her knowledge to discover new ways to prevent malaria. She helped health leaders share information about how the disease spread in their communities. Together, they created better health procedures across Africa—sometimes eliminating diseases entirely.

When a disease is eliminated, it means that treatments and vaccines are so effective that people no longer get it. While trying to eliminate malaria, Rose also faced another disease head-on. Polio had been eliminated in other countries, such as the United States, but it was still common in some countries in Africa. Along with other health leaders, Rose worked hard to accurately test communities for polio and offer more vaccines in areas with the most need. For countries like Nigeria, the program was a success! For two years, the country was free of the polio virus.

Using science, persistence, and community connections, Rose is working to ensure that diseases like polio and malaria become things of the past.

BORN FEBRUARY 13, 1947

CAMEROON

SOPHIE GERMAIN

MATHEMATICIAN

Long ago, a child named Sophie wanted to learn math, but her parents didn't think it was a proper subject for girls to study. They hid Sophie's candles, took her warm clothes, and put out her fire so she couldn't read math books at night. But after everyone else went to bed, Sophie would bundle up in a quilt, light a candle from her secret stash, and keep learning. When Sophie's parents found her shivering at her desk with a frozen inkwell, they realized nothing could stop their daughter's curiosity.

Women weren't allowed to attend universities at the time, but Sophie read notes from a college math class on her own. She even submitted homework, signing it with a man's name: Monsieur Le Blanc. When the professor discovered the truth—that this talented student was a woman—he was amazed.

A few years later, the French Academy of Sciences announced a math contest to help explain a puzzling phenomenon: if someone sprinkles powder on a plate and vibrates it, why do certain patterns form? Sophie worked on the problem for two years and submitted an answer. Sadly, the Academy said her math didn't add up. Two years later, she tried again. Her answer was still wrong.

After working on the same question for six years, Sophie tried one last time. The problem was so difficult that no one else had even bothered submitting an answer. But this time, Sophie had solved it! She received the grand prize of 3,000 francs and became the first woman in history to win a math competition. Sophie showed the world that math is a proper subject for girls to study—and that women can become brilliant mathematicians!

APRIL 1, 1776 – JUNE 27, 1831

FRANCE

VALENTINA MUÑOZ RABANAL

ACTIVIST AND PROGRAMMER

Once upon a time in Chile, there lived a girl named Valentina who spent a lot of time doing 3D puzzles. At an early age, Valentina dreamed of using her computer science skills to help save the world. At her public school, Valentina was able to join the competitive robotics team. She couldn't wait! There she learned how to build robots using LEGO bricks, and she became a three-time champion of the biggest international robotics competition.

Valentina knew that access to the online world was necessary for learning and working in STEM. She also knew that she was lucky. She thought about the millions of girls around the world who didn't have the same opportunities she had.

In Chile, there were far more boys than girls in STEM. Part of the problem was that girls weren't always treated equally by teachers. Even though Valentina was a LEGO champion, the male teacher who was in charge of the robotics team did not treat the girls in his class fairly, especially not Valentina. That was when it hit her: this was her chance to make a difference in the world, just like she'd been dreaming about ever since she was a kid.

Valentina and her friend started the Association of Young Women for Ideas, an organization for girls and by girls. The goal was to empower girls to learn about technology, the internet, and other STEM subjects. Thanks to activists like Valentina, the gap between girls and boys in STEM is closing every day!

BORN JULY 21, 2002

CHILE

MEET MORE REBELS

In the Good Night Stories for Rebel Girls series, we celebrate the accomplishments of many women and girls in STEM fields.

ANGELLA DOROTHEA FERGUSON

When Angella became a doctor, most medical research focused on white children, not Black children. Angella's trailblazing work changed that.

Illustration by Lydia Mba

EARYN MCGEE

Once there was a warm-hearted young woman with a cold-blooded fascination: reptiles! Earyn posts pictures of camouflaged lizards and challenges people to find them.

Illustration by Shiane Salabie

ESTHER OKADE

Once upon a time, Esther became one of the United Kingdom's youngest college students. She enrolled in college to study math when she was 10.

Illustration by Jenin Mohammed

FLORENCE NIGHTINGALE

Known as the founder of modern nursing, Florence made sure her patients were well taken care of and that their surroundings were safe and clean.

Illustration by Dalila Rovazzini

GITANJALI RAO

When Gitanjali learned that the residents of Flint, Michigan, didn't have clean water, she invented a sensor to detect pollution and send the results to people's phones.

Illustration by Amy Phelps

GRACE HOPPER

Grace used the first computer to help the US Army decode secret enemy messages during World War II.

Illustration by Kiki Ljung

JANE GOODALL

Other primatologists studied chimps in cages, but Jane got to know them in the wild. Thanks to her, we know more about these incredible creatures.

Illustration by Emmanuelle Walker

56

JOY BUOLAMWINI

Joy noticed that robots could identify white faces better than Black faces. She fights for proper representation of Black women in new technology.

Illustration by
Simone Martin-Newberry

JUDIT GIRÓ BENET

Judit's invention uses a simple urine sample to detect breast cancer in women. The device studies the sample, then sends the results to an app on the user's phone.

Illustration by
Jiawen Chen

JULIE RAZAFIMANAHAKA

When Julie heard the wailing song of the indri lemur, she was blown away. As a conservation biologist, she is determined to save these remarkable animals from extinction.

Illustration by
Shiane Salabie

KATHY HANNUN

Kathy knew using fossil fuels was hurting the planet. So she created a company that warms buildings using the natural heat found under Earth's surface instead.

Illustration by
Fabiola F. Aldrete Solorio

KATIA KRAFFT

Once there was a woman who loved volcanoes. Katia became a volcanologist and studied lava and eruptions up close.

Illustration by
Martina Paukova

LAUREN ESPOSITO

Lauren is an arachnologist who studies scorpions. She also runs the 500 Queer Scientists campaign, supporting scientists in the LGBTQIA+ community.

Illustration by
Maju Bengel

MAE JEMISON

Once upon a time, there was a curious girl named Mae who could not make up her mind about what she wanted to be when she grew up. She became the first Black woman in space.

Illustration by
Alexandra Bowman

MARCELA CONTRERAS

Marcela's leadership made sure that donated blood was always available to people who needed it after surgery, illness, or accidents—no matter where they lived.

Illustration by
Karina Coco

MARIE CURIE

Marie discovered two new chemical elements and became the first woman to receive a Nobel Prize.

Illustration by
Claudia Carieri

MARIE THARP

Geologist Marie became the first person ever to piece together a map of the mountains and valleys on the Atlantic seafloor.

Illustration by
Barbara Dziadosz

MARY ANNING

Mary loved walking by the sea, where she dug for fossils. Her discoveries helped prove that there has been life on our planet for hundreds of millions of years.

Illustration by
Martina Paukova

PURNIMA DEVI BARMAN

Purnima was studying ecology and wildlife biology when she learned that the hargila, a type of stork, was losing its habitat. She brought her community together to save the birds.

Illustration by
Jui Talukder

RESHMA KOSARAJU

Reshma was tired of living with the effects of wildfires in her home state of California. So she created a computer program to predict when fires would occur.

Illustration by
Avani Dwivedi

RITA LEVI-MONTALCINI

Even when Rita was forced into hiding during World War II because she was Jewish, she never gave up on her medical research. After the war, she won a Nobel Prize!

Illustration by
Cristina Amodeo

ROSALIND FRANKLIN

Rosalind discovered the shape of DNA, a molecule that tells the body how to develop and function. But she didn't get full credit for her work until after she died.

Illustration by
Liekeland

ROSELI OCAMPO-FRIEDMANN

Once there was a girl who was fascinated by plants that lived in odd places. Roseli grew up to discover microorganisms in Antarctica and Siberia.

Illustration by
Sally Caulwell

SARA MAZROUEI

As a planetary geologist, Sara teaches others about space and studies things like the history of asteroids and the best landing locations for future lunar missions.

Illustration by
Eva Rust

SAU LAN WU

Sau Lan got a PhD in physics and went on to study the tiny particles that make up atoms, which in turn make up everything else in the universe.

Illustration by
Adriana Bellet

SYLVIA EARLE

Once upon a time, there was a marine biologist named Sylvia who loved to dive at night, when she could study fish she couldn't see during the day.

Illustration by
Geraldine Sy

TEMPLE GRANDIN

Temple has autism, and her way of thinking helped her understand how animals see the world. She is a world-famous professor of animal sciences.

Illustration by
Janie Secker

VELMA SCANTLEBURY

Physician Velma has performed more than 2,000 transplant surgeries and has won many awards for her work.

Illustration by
Irene Rinaldi

VICTORIA ALONSOPEREZ

When a disease was spreading among cows in Uruguay, where Victoria lived, she created a product that helped farmers track their livestock's health.

Illustration by
Natalia Cardona Puerta

WANG ZHENYI

In the 1700s, people thought a lunar eclipse was a sign that the gods were angry. Astronomer Zhenyi proved how eclipses really worked.

Illustration by
Ana Galvañ

YOKY MATSUOKA

Robotics engineer Yoky built mechanical arms that could help people learn to use their muscles again after a stroke.

Illustration by
Lisa Lanoe

KEEP INNOVATING

TELL YOUR TALE

It's time to explore the Rebel you know the best—you! All you need is a piece of paper, something to write and draw with, and your imagination.

- Fold a piece of paper in half on the long end, like a book, then unfold it.

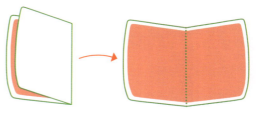

- Think about how you want to tell your story. What would you want readers to know about you if you were featured in a Rebel Girls book?
- On the left side of the fold, write your name in big bright letters. Then write your story.

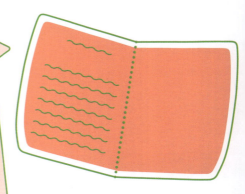

STORYTELLING TIPS
There are lots of ways to tell your story.
- You can start with "Once upon a time..." like in Darshan Ranganathan's story or jump right into the action like in Irene Uchida's.
- Consider telling a story about when you were little or sharing a moment when you were extra proud of yourself.
- Make sure to add lots of details.
- If you are describing a moment in your life, close your eyes and remember what that moment was like. Then describe what it looked like, how it smelled, and the sounds you heard.

DRAW YOUR PORTRAIT

Channel your inner artist and make a self-portrait, or picture of yourself.

1. What materials would you like to use? Colored pencils? Crayons? Pens? Watercolors? Would you like to draw or paint? Gather your supplies.
2. On the right side of the fold, draw your portrait.

UNiQUE YOU

Every self-portrait is different. What do you want your picture to show?

- You can show yourself posing like Nicole Aunapu Mann or doing an activity like Etheldred Benett.
- You can focus on your face or show yourself from your head to your feet — or anything in between.
- The portrait can be realistic or abstract, colorful or black and white — however you see yourself.
- Don't forget the background! It can also be realistic or abstract. What does the background of your portrait share about you?

3. When you're done, you can share your story and portrait with a friend or family member, hang it up, or even keep it tucked inside this book.

MEMORiZE Pi

Emma Haruka Iwao calculated 100 trillion digits of pi. Nobody can remember that many numbers, but challenge yourself to see how many you can memorize.

1. With an adult's permission, go online and look up the digits of pi. You can use a site like piday.org/million, which lists the first million digits of pi.
2. See how many you can remember. You can try strategies like:
   - Setting the digits to the tune of a song you like
   - Breaking the digits you want to memorize into shorter chunks. Once you have a chunk memorized, add another chunk, then another, and see how far you can get.
   - Writing a poem that rhymes with a string of numbers, like:
     3.14159
     Hold those numbers in your mind.
     265358
     What comes next? I can't wait!
3. Once you've memorized as many digits as you can, share with a friend or family member. You can even have a competition to see who can remember the most.

WRiTE AN OUTER SPACE PACKiNG LiST

When Nicole Aunapu Mann went to space, she brought her dream catcher with her. What would you bring on an interstellar journey?

1. Think about a few things you'd definitely need to take with you. Nicole stayed up in space for a few months. What food, clothes, and other necessities would you want to have for that amount of time?
2. Next, think about some items, like Nicole's dream catcher, that might not be necessary for survival but would be important for you to have by your side. You might choose a favorite stuffed animal, a photo of your family, or anything else that might remind you of home.
3. Write up your list. You can even draw a picture of yourself using some of your items in space.

MAKE YOUR OWN MANCALA BOARD

Nkechi Agwu grew up seeing math in games like mancala. You can create your own mancala board to play with your friends or family.

1. Ask an adult to help you cut the top off an empty egg carton so only the bottom remains. Use a carton that contained a dozen eggs so you have two rows of six cups.
2. Decorate the egg carton however you like. You can use stickers, paint, glitter, markers, or any other favorite craft supplies—just make sure to ask an adult for permission if you're using messy materials.
3. Find two larger cups to place at each short end of the egg carton.
4. Collect 24 small items or tokens that will fit easily into the small cups. You can use pennies, beads, jelly beans, Cheerios—whatever you like!
5. Place four pieces in each small cup, leaving the bigger cups on the ends empty.
6. With a grown-up's permission, look up directions for how to play mancala online. You may want to watch a YouTube tutorial to get a feel for it. There are lots of different variations—pick your favorite or try out a few.
7. Find someone to play with, and let the games begin!

SEARCH FOR ROCKS

Etheldred Benett scoured the countryside around her home for fossils. What kinds of rocks can you find near where you live?

1. In your backyard or a park near your home, spend some time looking for rocks. You can use a stick, a plastic spoon, or a small shovel to help you search in the dirt. Make sure you ask permission before digging too deeply.
2. Once you have as many rocks as you'd like to collect, brush or rinse any dirt off of them.
3. Make some observations. What do the rocks look like? Are they smooth or jagged? Are they small or large? Are they shiny or dull? Do they all look similar, or do they seem like different types? What colors can you see?
4. Write down your observations or make sketches in a notebook.
5. When you're done, you can keep the rocks for your collection or put them back outside for another explorer to find.

DESIGN A ROBOT

Cynthia Breazeal's robots work to make humans' lives easier. If you were designing your own robot, what would it do?

1. Brainstorm what problem you want to solve with your robot. Maybe you want it to help you load the dishwasher or clean up your room. Maybe you want it to clear off the sidewalk in front of you while you're walking to school on icy days. Use your imagination!
2. Make a list of the features the robot would need to have in order to solve your problem. If you were creating a dishwasher-loading robot, for example, it would need to be tall enough to reach the sink and strong enough to hold on to the dishes. You might want it to be waterproof, too, so it can prerinse the plates.
3. Once you have a good idea of what you want your robot to do, sketch out how you'd like it to look. Will it be obvious it's a robot, or will it look like something else?
4. Flesh out your drawing with colored pencils or markers. You can even build a prototype out of paper or clay if you'd like.
5. When you're happy with your design, show it to a friend or family member and explain your idea. Can you convince them that the world needs your robot?

CODE YOUR NAME

Computer scientists like Lynn Conway use code to give computers directions and represent words and numbers. Learn to write your name using binary code, a simple system of zeroes and ones.

Binary Alphabet	
A 1000001	**N** 1001110
B 1000010	**O** 1001111
C 1000011	**P** 1010000
D 1000100	**Q** 1010001
E 1000101	**R** 1010010
F 1000110	**S** 1010011
G 1000111	**T** 1010100
H 1001000	**U** 1010101
I 1001001	**V** 1010110
J 1001010	**W** 1010111
K 1001011	**X** 1010111
L 1001100	**Y** 1011001
M 1001101	**Z** 1011010

1. Using this chart, find the binary code symbols that correspond to each letter of your name.
2. On a separate sheet of paper, write your name using binary code. What's it like to write in these symbols instead of the regular alphabet?
3. If you were creating your own code, what symbol would you use for each letter of the alphabet? Create your own system and then use it to write your name, a friend's name, or any other word you'd like.

LiSTEN TO MORE EMPOWERiNG STORiES ON THE REBEL GiRLS APP!

Download the app to listen to beloved Rebel Girls stories. Filled with the adventures and accomplishments of women from around the world and throughout history, the Rebel Girls app is designed to entertain, inspire, and build confidence in listeners everywhere.

THE ILLUSTRATORS

Twenty extraordinary female artists from all over the world illustrated the portraits in this book.

BRiA NiCOLE, **USA**, 49
CAiTLiN RAiN, **USA**, 23
CAMiLLA RU, **UK**, 51
CARO MARTíNEZ "CHABASKi", **MEXiCO**, 35
DONG QiU, **CHiNA**, 15
ELiSABETTA STOiNiCH, **ITALY**, 7
FARiMAH KHAVARiNEZHAD, **CANADA**, 41
JULiETTE TOMA, **USA**, 37
KELSEE THOMAS, **USA**, 19
KiMBERLiE CLiNTHORNE-WONG, **USA**, 25, 27
MARTiNA BRANCATO, **ITALY**, 53

MiCHELLE R. D'URBANO, **ZAMBiA**, 47
MONET ALYSSA, **USA**, 31, 43
NiCOLE NEiDHARDT, **USA AND CANADA**, 39
STORY HEMi-MOREHOUSE, **NEW ZEALAND**, 29, 45
TiNA MEi, **USA**, 9
TRiSHA SRiVASTAVA, **INDiA**, 17
VALERiA ARAYA, **CHiLE**, 13, 55
VERONiCA JOHNSON, **USA**, 33
YiYi CHEN, **USA**, 11, 21

MORE BOOKS!

For more stories about amazing women and girls, check out other Rebel Girls books.

ABOUT REBEL GIRLS

REBEL GiRLS, a certified B Corporation, is a global, multi-platform empowerment brand dedicated to helping raise the most inspired and confident generation of girls through content, experiences, products, and community. Originating from an international best-selling children's book, Rebel Girls amplifies stories of real-life, extraordinary women throughout history, geography, and field of excellence. With a growing community of 35 million self-identified Rebel Girls spanning more than 100 countries, the brand engages with Generation Alpha through its book series, premier app and audio content, events, and merchandise. To date, Rebel Girls has sold more than 11 million books in 50 languages and reached 55 million audio listens. Award recognition includes the *New York Times* bestseller list, the 2022 Apple Design Award for Social Impact, multiple Webby Awards for Family, Kids & Education, and Common Sense Media Selection honors, among many others.

As a B Corp, we're part of a global community of businesses that meet high standards of social and environmental impact.

JOiN THE REBEL GiRLS COMMUNiTY!
Visit rebelgirls.com and join our email list for exclusive sneak peeks, promos, activities, and more. You can also email us at hello@rebelgirls.com.
- ✦ YouTube: youtube.com/RebelGirls
- ✦ App: rebelgirls.com/audio
- ✦ Podcast: rebelgirls.com/podcast
- ✦ Facebook: facebook.com/rebelgirls
- ✦ Instagram: @rebelgirls
- ✦ Email: hello@rebelgirls.com
- ✦ Web: rebelgirls.com

If you liked this book, please take a moment to review it wherever you prefer!